Introduction: Unveiling the Adventure

Dear young explorers, welcome to the exciting journey that awaits within the pages of "A Kids Guide to Being Totally American." In this vibrant handbook, we embark on an adventure to unravel the essence of what it truly means to be American through the eyes of the youthful spirit.

America is more than just a place on the map; it's a tapestry woven with threads of diversity, dreams, and the shared pursuit of happiness. Whether you're gazing at the stars and stripes, savoring a classic American snack, cheering at a school event, or making a new friend, each experience contributes to the grand mosaic that is being totally American.

This guide is not a rulebook but a compass, offering glimpses into the whimsical, the heartfelt, and the everyday aspects of American life. From the casual "Hi!" that echoes across neighborhoods to the joyous celebrations that bring communities together, we'll explore the nuances that make being totally American an ongoing adventure.

Throughout these pages, you'll discover the magic of school spirit, the dynamic language of super slang, the thrill of healthy competition on the sports field, and the joy of learning in the realm of homework heroes. Each chapter is a portal into a different facet of the American experience, a chance to celebrate the unique blend of cultures, traditions, and friendships that shape our collective journey.

So, young adventurers, fasten your seatbelts and prepare for a whimsical ride through the heart of America. Let's smile, say hi, share a snack, and navigate the colorful landscape of being totally American together. The adventure unfolds, and the pages are waiting to be turned. Welcome, dear explorers, to the enchanting world of being totally American!

Chapter 1: Smile and Say Hi!

In America, folks love to greet each other with a smile and a friendly "hi" or "hello." Practice your friendly waves, and soon you'll be fitting right in!

Chapter 2: Snack Attack!

Learn the art of snacking on classic American treats. Whether it's popcorn at the movies or a PB&J sandwich, tasty snacks are a key to blending in with your new pals.

Chapter 3: Dress for Success

Discover the cool styles of American fashion! From jeans and sneakers to T-shirts with funny sayings, dressing like your friends helps you feel comfy and look awesome.

Chapter 4: School Spirit

Get into the spirit of school! Join in on fun activities, cheer for the home team, and maybe even wear a cap with your school's logo. School pride is a surefire way to make friends.

Chapter 5: Super Slang

Catch onto some easy-peasy American slang! Words like "cool" and "awesome" are like secret codes for fitting in. Try using them, and soon you'll be talking like a true American kiddo!

Chapter 6: Celebrate Together

Join in on celebrations like birthdays, Halloween, and Thanksgiving. Participate in games, wear costumes, and share yummy treats. Everyone loves a good celebration, and you will too!

Chapter 7: Be a Good Sport

Learn the rules of popular American sports like soccer, basketball, or baseball. Cheering for a team and playing sports with your new friends is a fantastic way to be part of the action.

Chapter 8: Speak Up!

Practice speaking up in class and sharing your ideas. Americans love to hear what you think! Don't be shy; your thoughts are just as important as everyone else's.

Chapter 9: Homework Heroes

Show your smarts by tackling your homework with a can-do attitude. Studying and doing your best in school are great ways to impress your teachers and classmates.

Chapter 10: Be a Good Friend

Last but not least, be a good friend! Share toys, listen when others talk, and help out when someone needs a hand. Being kind is the ultimate secret to fitting in wherever you are!

Remember, blending in is all about having fun, being yourself, and making friends along the way. So, put on that big smile, get ready for some high-fives, and enjoy your adventure in America!

Chapter 1: Smile and Say Hi!

Welcome to the exciting adventure of becoming totally American! In this first chapter, we'll dive into a key aspect of American culture that sets the stage for friendly interactions and positive vibes—smiling and saying hi.

 In the United States, a warm smile is like a universal language. It's a way to spread joy, show kindness, and create a welcoming atmosphere. Whether you're meeting someone new, passing by a neighbor, or entering a room, a genuine smile can brighten the day for both you and those around you.

Now, let's talk about the magic of saying hi. In America, greeting people with a friendly "hi" or "hello" is more than just a formality; it's a way to acknowledge others and build connections. It's like a little burst of sunshine in your day. So, don't be shy—give it a try!

Imagine you're walking into a classroom, and you see your classmates. A simple "hi" or a cheerful wave can create a positive start to your day. It's an easy way to show that you're friendly and approachable.

But it's not just about the words; it's about the energy you bring. A smile and a friendly greeting can break the ice, making people feel comfortable and happy to be around you. It's the first step in building a community where everyone feels included and valued.

In some cultures, people may not greet each other as openly, but in America, saying hi is like extending a hand in friendship. It's a small gesture that can have a big impact, making you feel connected to the people around you.

So, whether you're at school, in your neighborhood, or exploring a new place, remember the golden rule of Chapter One: Smile and say hi! It's a simple yet powerful way to embrace the spirit of friendliness and openness that makes being totally American so special.

As you embark on this journey, let your smile be a beacon of positivity, and your greetings be the start of countless friendships. The adventure has just begun, and with a smile on your face and a friendly "hi" on your lips, you're well on your way to mastering the art of being totally American!

Chapter 2: Snack Attack

Get ready, young explorer, because in Chapter Two, we're diving into a realm that's as American as apple pie—the delightful world of snacks! Welcome to "Snack Attack," where we'll uncover the tasty treasures that make snack time a beloved part of being totally American.

Snacking isn't just about satisfying your hunger; it's a cherished pastime, a flavorful journey through an array of delicious options that cater to every taste bud. From savory to sweet, crunchy to chewy, the world of American snacks is as diverse as the country itself.

Let's start with the classics. Picture yourself at a baseball game, cheering for your favorite team. What snack do you have in hand? It's likely a bag of popcorn, buttery and salty, the perfect companion for a thrilling game. Popcorn has been a staple of American snacking for generations, bringing joy and crunchiness to movie nights, carnivals, and cozy gatherings.

Now, let's talk about the iconic duo—chips and dip. Whether it's crispy potato chips with tangy onion dip or tortilla chips paired with zesty salsa, this dynamic duo is a snack-time sensation. The variety of flavors and textures is a testament to the creative spirit that defines American snacking.

Of course, no exploration of American snacks would be complete without a nod to the beloved peanut butter and jelly sandwich. It's not just a lunchtime favorite; it's a timeless classic that captures the essence of comfort and simplicity. The marriage of creamy peanut butter and fruity jelly between two slices of bread is a snack masterpiece enjoyed by kids and grown-ups alike.

But wait, there's more! Dive into the world of sweet treats with cookies, brownies, and candies. Chocolate chip cookies, with their gooey centers and crispy edges, have a special place in the hearts of snack enthusiasts. And who could resist the allure of a fudgy brownie or the joy of unwrapping a piece of candy, each bite a burst of sweetness?

Let's not forget the beverage scene. From refreshing fruit juices to the quintessential American drink—cola—snack time often comes with a drink in hand. The sound of a can opening or the fizz of bubbles in a glass adds an extra layer of enjoyment to the snacking experience.

The beauty of "Snack Attack" goes beyond the flavors. It's about the shared moments of joy, whether you're swapping snacks with friends at a sleepover or discovering a new treat with family. Snacking is a social activity, a chance to bond over a shared love for tasty delights and create memories that last a lifetime.

As you navigate the exciting landscape of American snacks, remember that variety is the spice of snack life. Embrace the diversity of flavors, try new combinations, and savor each bite. "Snack Attack" isn't just about filling your stomach; it's about indulging in the simple pleasures that make being totally American a delicious adventure.

So, young snacker, let your taste buds be your guide as you explore the world of snacks. From the crunch of chips to the sweetness of cookies, may your snack adventures be as delightful as the treats themselves. Snack on, little explorer, and enjoy every tasty moment of being totally American!

Chapter 3: Dress for Success

In the lively journey of being totally American, Chapter Three invites young adventurers to step into the world of fashion and discover the art of "Dress for Success." It's more than just picking out clothes; it's about expressing yourself, embracing diversity, and feeling confident in what you wear.

American fashion is a vibrant tapestry, woven with threads of individuality and cultural influences from all over the world. Whether you're heading to school, a special event, or just a day of fun, what you wear is a canvas for self-expression.

First, let's talk about the iconic denim jeans. As American as apple pie, jeans are a staple in every wardrobe. They're versatile, comfortable, and come in a rainbow of styles. From classic blue to trendy colors and patterns, jeans allow you to showcase your personality while staying comfy on the go.

For special occasions, dressing up can be a thrilling adventure. Picture yourself twirling in a dress or strutting in a sharp suit. Whether it's a family celebration or a school dance, the right outfit can make you feel like the star of the show. Remember, dressing for success isn't just about fancy clothes; it's about wearing what makes you feel confident and ready to conquer the day.

Footwear plays a crucial role in the American fashion landscape. Sneakers are more than just shoes; they're a statement. Whether you're running around at the playground or joining friends for a game, sneakers are your trusty companions. And for those special moments, a shiny pair of shoes can add a touch of elegance to your ensemble.

Hats, sunglasses, and accessories are like the sprinkles on the fashion cupcake. They add flair and personality to your look. A stylish hat or a pair of cool shades can turn a simple outfit into a fashion statement. It's all about finding the accessories that resonate with your style and make you feel uniquely you.

But here's the secret ingredient: confidence. No matter what you wear, wearing it with confidence is the key to success. Your clothes are an extension of your personality, and when you feel good in them, it shows. So, stand tall, walk with purpose, and let your outfit be a reflection of the awesome person you are.

"Dress for Success" is not about following strict rules; it's about celebrating your individuality. In the diverse tapestry of America, fashion is a way to express your identity, embrace cultural influences, and celebrate the rich mosaic of styles that make up this nation.

As you navigate the exciting world of American fashion, remember that being totally American means being true to yourself. So, open your closet, explore different styles, and let your outfit be a canvas for the unique masterpiece that is you. Dress for success, young fashionista, and let your style shine bright in the wonderful adventure of being totally American!

Chapter 4: School Spirit

Ahoy, young scholars! Chapter Four invites you to dive headfirst into the spirited realm of "School Spirit." It's more than just cheering at games; it's a lively celebration of community, camaraderie, and the pride that comes with being part of something bigger—your school family.

School spirit is like a magical force that brings everyone together. It's the energy that buzzes through the hallways during pep rallies, the roar of excitement at sports events, and the creative enthusiasm of spirit week. So, grab your pom-poms and let's explore the vibrant world of school spirit!

First things first—sports events. Whether it's a basketball game, a football match, or a track meet, school spirit shines bright in the stands. Decked out in your school colors, you become a vital part of the cheering squad. The sound of cheers, chants, and the rhythmic claps creates an electric atmosphere that fuels the team's energy.

But school spirit isn't limited to athletics. It extends to academic achievements, artistic endeavors, and the everyday victories of learning and growing together. Celebrating achievements, big or small, fosters a sense of unity and pride in your school community.

Spirit week is like a festive holiday in the school calendar. Each day brings a new theme—crazy hat day, pajama day, or even superhero day. It's a chance to unleash your creativity, express yourself, and bond with your classmates in a whirlwind of themed fun. Plus, who doesn't love a good costume parade?

Now, let's talk about the heart of school spirit—the mascot. Whether it's a roaring lion, a spirited eagle, or any other symbol representing your school, the mascot is the embodiment of pride and enthusiasm. Cheering alongside the mascot at events creates a lively and memorable experience for everyone involved.

Beyond the events and the cheers, school spirit is about fostering a sense of belonging. It's creating an inclusive environment where every student feels valued and supported. Acts of kindness, encouraging words, and a positive attitude contribute to the vibrant tapestry of school spirit.

And of course, let's not forget the iconic school apparel. Whether it's a cozy hoodie, a spirited T-shirt, or a colorful scarf, wearing your school gear is a visual declaration of your connection to the school family. It's like wearing your heart on your sleeve—or in this case, your school colors!

School spirit is a collective adventure, and everyone plays a part. So, whether you're a cheerleader, an athlete, an artist, or a bookworm, your unique contributions make the school spirit thrive. It's the shared memories, the laughter, and the friendships formed along the way that create the spirited essence of being totally American in school.

As you navigate the spirited halls of academia, let your enthusiasm shine. Cheer loud, create memories, and embrace the lively world of school spirit. Being totally American in school is not just about academics; it's about embracing the vibrant community that becomes your second home. So, young scholar, let your school spirit soar high, and let the adventures continue in the joyful journey of being totally American!

Chapter 5: Super Slang

Slang is like the secret code of cool kids, a dynamic language that evolves with the times. It's the key to unlocking a sense of belonging and a way to sprinkle your conversations with a dash of personality. So, get ready to unleash your linguistic superpowers as we explore the ever-changing landscape of American slang.

First on our linguistic journey is the phrase "cool." It's not just a temperature; it's the ultimate seal of approval. When something is cool, it's awesome, fantastic, or just downright impressive. Whether you're describing a new gadget, a rad skateboard trick, or a friend's snazzy outfit, "cool" is the go-to expression.

Now, let's talk about "chill." It's not just a relaxing vibe; it's a state of mind. When things are chill, they're easygoing, laid-back, and stress-free. Picture a weekend with friends, a leisurely day at the park, or a movie night with a bowl of popcorn—those are all moments when things are totally chill.

And who could forget "awesome sauce"? This playful expression takes "awesome" to a whole new level. It's like adding a secret ingredient to your enthusiasm, making your excitement extra special. When you accomplish something great or witness an epic moment, you can't help but exclaim, "That's awesome sauce!"

But wait, there's more! The term "lit" is like the spark that ignites a fire of excitement. When a party is lit, a performance is lit, or even a piece of artwork is lit, it means it's on fire with energy, enthusiasm, and all-around awesomeness. It's a slang term that adds a burst of flavor to your descriptions.

Moving on to "snazzy," this word is like a stylish superhero in the slang universe. When something is snazzy, it's sharp, stylish, and eye-catching. Whether it's a new pair of sneakers, a cool haircut, or a dazzling outfit, calling it snazzy is a surefire way to express admiration.

And now, let's talk about "bae." This term is not just a cute sound; it's an endearing way to refer to someone special. Short for "before anyone else," bae is the slang equivalent of saying, "You're my number one." It's a sweet expression of affection that adds a touch of romance to everyday language.

Super slang is like a dynamic dance of words, a linguistic playground where expressions morph and adapt to reflect the spirit of the times. As you navigate the world of American slang, remember that language is a living, breathing entity. Embrace the playful phrases, experiment with expressions, and let your words be a reflection of your unique linguistic style.

So, young language aficionado, dive into the lexicon of super slang, where every word is a superhero in its own right. Whether you're describing a fantastic day, an incredible idea, or a fabulous friend, let the colorful world of super slang be your linguistic playground. After all, being totally American is not just about what you say; it's about how you say it. Awesome!

Chapter 6: Celebrate Together

Young revelers, Chapter Six beckons you to join the festive extravaganza of "Celebrate Together." It's more than just parties and parades; it's a vibrant exploration of the communal spirit that defines American celebrations. So, grab your party hats and get ready to dive into a whirlwind of festivities, traditions, and the joyous art of coming together.

Celebrations in America are a kaleidoscope of colors, flavors, and traditions, reflecting the rich tapestry of cultures that make up this nation. From Independence Day fireworks to Thanksgiving feasts, each celebration is a unique opportunity to connect with family, friends, and the wider community.

Let's kick off our celebration journey with the explosive brilliance of Independence Day. Picture a sky adorned with bursts of red, white, and blue as fireworks paint a spectacular canvas. Independence Day is more than just a commemoration of history; it's a nationwide party, a time when communities gather to celebrate freedom, unity, and the spirit of being totally American.

Moving on to Thanksgiving, this holiday is like a grand feast that brings families together around the table. The aroma of roasted turkey, the warmth of shared stories, and the chorus of laughter create an atmosphere of gratitude. Thanksgiving is a time to reflect on blessings, appreciate the company of loved ones, and indulge in a delicious feast that showcases the flavors of the season.

But celebrations in America aren't confined to national holidays. Picture a birthday party filled with balloons, cake, and the chorus of "Happy Birthday." Birthdays are a special time to celebrate individuality, mark milestones, and shower friends with joy and presents. It's a personal celebration that adds sparkle to the tapestry of American festivities.

As we delve into the vibrant world of cultural celebrations, the Festival of Lights during Diwali illuminates neighborhoods with the warm glow of diyas. Lunar New Year festivities paint the streets red with vibrant decorations and dragon dances, symbolizing good fortune and new beginnings. These celebrations highlight the diversity woven into the fabric of America, offering a glimpse into the customs that make each community unique.

Now, let's talk about parades—the lively processions that bring communities together. Whether it's a hometown parade on the Fourth of July or a spectacular display during a cultural festival, parades are a visual symphony of floats, music, and the cheerful wave of spectators. They embody the collective spirit of celebration, uniting individuals in shared joy.

The beauty of "Celebrate Together" lies in its inclusivity. It's an open invitation for everyone to join the festivities, regardless of background or beliefs. It's a reminder that, in the tapestry of America, each thread contributes to the vibrant mosaic of celebrations. Whether it's a block party, a community fair, or a cultural festival, coming together to celebrate strengthens the bonds that connect us all.

As you embark on the adventure of "Celebrate Together," cherish the moments of joy, savor the flavors of tradition, and relish the shared laughter that echoes through celebrations. Whether you're dancing in the glow of fireworks, sharing a festive meal, or waving at the colorful floats in a parade, remember that being totally American is about embracing the communal spirit that makes celebrations truly special.

So, young reveler, let the spirit of celebration be your guide. Dance to the rhythm of shared joy, savor the magic of traditions, and relish the moments when we all come together to celebrate the beautiful tapestry of being totally American.

Hey there, young athletes and sports enthusiasts! Chapter Seven ushers you onto the playing field of life with the vibrant theme of "Be a Good Sport." It's not just about winning or losing; it's about embracing the values of teamwork, sportsmanship, and the thrill of healthy competition. So, lace up your imaginary sneakers, grab your sportsmanship playbook, and let's dive into the world of being totally American in the realm of sports.

In America, sports aren't just games; they're a cultural phenomenon that brings communities together. Whether it's shooting hoops on the basketball court, scoring goals on the soccer field, or swinging for the fences on the baseball diamond, sports play a vital role in shaping character, building friendships, and fostering a sense of unity.

First and foremost, let's talk about teamwork. Being a good sport means recognizing that every player on the team plays a crucial role. It's about passing the ball, cheering on your teammates, and celebrating both individual and collective successes. The joy of victory is sweeter when shared with others, and the camaraderie formed on the field extends beyond the game itself.

But what about when things don't go as planned? That's where sportsmanship comes into play. Whether you win or lose, being a good sport means shaking hands with opponents, acknowledging their efforts, and showing respect. It's about understanding that, in the game of life, the lessons learned through wins and losses contribute to personal growth.

Now, let's talk about fair play. In the spirit of being totally American, fairness is a guiding principle on the sports field. It means playing by the rules, respecting referees and umpires, and embracing the concept of a level playing field. Fair play ensures that every player has an equal opportunity to showcase their skills and contribute to the excitement of the game.

But being a good sport extends beyond the field of play. It's about carrying the values of sportsmanship into everyday life. Whether you're participating in a school project, engaging in friendly competitions, or navigating challenges, the principles of teamwork, respect, and fair play remain constant.

The beauty of "Be a Good Sport" is that it transcends individual sports and encompasses a wide range of activities. Whether you're sprinting on a track, executing a perfect dive, or even engaging in a spirited game of chess, the principles of being a good sport apply. It's about the spirit of competition, the thrill of challenge, and the joy of participation.

Sports have a unique ability to unite people from diverse backgrounds, fostering a sense of community and shared purpose. Whether you're a star player, a dedicated fan, or someone exploring different sports, being a good sport is a mindset that adds richness to the experience.

So, young athletes, embrace the lessons of "Be a Good Sport" with open arms. Whether you're dribbling a basketball, scoring a touchdown, or simply playing catch with friends, let the values of sportsmanship guide your actions. After all, being totally American in the world of sports is not just about the game; it's about the character you bring to the field and the lasting impact you leave on those around you. Play on, young sports enthusiasts, and revel in the joy of being a good sport!

Chapter 8: Speak Up

Hey there, young voices ready to be heard! Chapter Eight invites you to step into the dynamic arena of "Speak Up." It's not just about making noise; it's about finding your voice, expressing your thoughts, and embracing the power of communication. So, grab your metaphorical microphone, stand tall, and let's explore the world of being totally American through the art of speaking up.

In the vast tapestry of America, the ability to speak up is like a vibrant thread that weaves through the fabric of democracy, community, and individual expression. From classrooms to community meetings, from family discussions to the public square, speaking up is a fundamental aspect of being an active and engaged member of society.

First and foremost, let's talk about the classroom. Whether you're sharing ideas during a group project, asking questions during a lesson, or participating in a class discussion, speaking up in school is a powerful way to contribute to the learning environment. Your thoughts and perspectives matter, and by expressing them, you not only enhance your own understanding but also enrich the collective knowledge of the class.

Now, let's venture into the realm of community. Town hall meetings, neighborhood gatherings, and community events provide opportunities for individuals to speak up and contribute to the well-being of the community. Whether it's expressing concerns, sharing ideas for improvement, or celebrating achievements, your voice plays a vital role in shaping the communities we call home.

But speaking up is not just about formal settings; it's also about everyday conversations. Sharing your thoughts, feelings, and experiences with family and friends fosters connection and understanding. It's a way to build strong relationships, support one another, and create a sense of unity within your personal circles.

Speaking up is not only about expressing agreement; it's about voicing dissent when necessary. In America, the freedom to express differing opinions is a cornerstone of democracy. It's the recognition that diverse perspectives contribute to a more robust and inclusive society. So, don't be afraid to respectfully challenge ideas, engage in constructive dialogue, and contribute to the ongoing conversations that shape the nation.

As you navigate the world of "Speak Up," remember that your voice is unique and valuable. Whether you're advocating for positive change, sharing your passions, or standing up for what you believe in, your voice has the power to make a difference. Embrace the confidence to speak up, knowing that your words contribute to the ever-evolving narrative of what it means to be totally American.

So, young communicators, let the spirit of "Speak Up" be your guide. Whether you're expressing yourself in the classroom, contributing to community discussions, or engaging in meaningful conversations with those around you, let your voice resonate with the confidence that comes from being totally American. Speak up, young advocates, and let your words echo in the wonderful journey of self-expression and community engagement!

Greetings, young scholars and knowledge seekers! Chapter Nine invites you to embark on an academic adventure as "Homework Heroes." It's not just about completing assignments; it's about embracing the journey of learning, cultivating good study habits, and unlocking the superhero potential within every student. So, grab your metaphorical capes, sharpen your pencils, and let's dive into the world of being totally American through the lens of academic excellence.

In the United States, education is not just a pathway; it's a cornerstone of individual growth and societal progress. "Homework Heroes" celebrates the pursuit of knowledge, the joy of discovery, and the satisfaction that comes from conquering academic challenges.

First and foremost, let's talk about the importance of setting a dedicated study space. Whether it's a cozy corner of your room, a well-lit desk, or a spot at the kitchen table, having a designated study area helps create a focused and conducive environment for learning. This is your superhero headquarters, where you unleash the power of concentration and dive into the exciting world of homework.

Now, let's explore the magical realm of organization. Homework heroes know the significance of keeping their tools in order. From notebooks and pens to textbooks and assignments, having an organized backpack and study materials ensures that you're ready to tackle any academic mission that comes your way. It's like having a superpower that wards off the chaos of clutter!

Homework heroes also understand the value of time management. Balancing homework, extracurricular activities, and personal time requires a bit of strategic planning. Creating a schedule, setting priorities, and allocating time for different tasks empower you to navigate the academic landscape with efficiency and ease. It's the superhero skill of juggling responsibilities with finesse.

But what about when you encounter challenges or face tough assignments? That's where the superpower of perseverance comes into play. Homework heroes don't shy away from difficulties; they embrace them as opportunities for growth. Whether it's seeking help from teachers, collaborating with classmates, or breaking down complex problems step by step, the ability to persevere is a hallmark of academic excellence.

Now, let's talk about the joy of curiosity. Homework heroes approach their assignments with a sense of wonder and inquisitiveness. They see homework not as a chore but as a chance to explore new ideas, deepen their understanding of the world, and develop a lifelong love for learning. The superhero mindset is fueled by the excitement of discovery!

In the world of "Homework Heroes," there's a recognition that every student has a unique set of strengths and talents. Whether you excel in mathematics, thrive in creative writing, or shine in scientific exploration, being a homework hero means embracing your individuality and using your strengths to contribute to the academic tapestry.

So, young scholars, let the spirit of "Homework Heroes" guide your academic journey. Whether you're tackling math problems, exploring the wonders of literature, or conducting scientific experiments, approach your homework with the enthusiasm and determination of a superhero on a mission. Homework heroes, the academic adventure awaits—embrace the challenge, unlock your potential, and let the joy of learning be your superpower in the quest of being totally American!

Chapter 10: Be a Good Friend

Ahoy, young adventurers in the realm of friendship! Chapter Ten extends an invitation to explore the heartwarming landscape of "Be a Good Friend." It's not just about companionship; it's about building bonds, practicing empathy, and navigating the exciting journey of human connection. So, gather 'round, my fellow explorers, and let's delve into the world of being totally American through the lens of friendship.

Friendship is like a treasure map with each friend marking a unique spot on the journey of life. In America, the diversity of friendships mirrors the rich tapestry of the nation itself. "Be a Good Friend" is an ode to the power of camaraderie, understanding, and the shared moments that make the adventure of friendship truly special.

First and foremost, let's talk about the superpower of listening. Being a good friend means lending an ear, offering a shoulder to lean on, and genuinely listening to the thoughts and feelings of others. The ability to hear, understand, and empathize forms the foundation of lasting friendships. It's a superpower that transforms ordinary moments into opportunities for connection.

Now, let's explore the essence of support. Good friends stand by each other through thick and thin. Whether it's cheering on achievements, providing comfort during challenging times, or simply being there for a laugh, the support of a good friend is a constant beacon of positivity. It's the superhero cape that shields against the storms of life.

But what about differences? In the diverse landscape of friendships, embracing individuality is a hallmark of being totally American. Good friends celebrate each other's uniqueness, learn from diverse perspectives, and create a space where everyone feels valued and accepted. It's the recognition that diversity adds richness to the tapestry of friendship.

The language of friendship Is not confined to words alone. Actions speak volumes, and good friends practice the art of kindness. Whether it's offering a helping hand, sharing a snack, or creating small surprises, acts of kindness strengthen the bonds of friendship. It's like sprinkling magic dust that adds warmth and joy to the shared journey.

Now, let's talk about the adventure of shared experiences. From playful escapades to deep conversations, good friends create memories that last a lifetime. Whether it's exploring the great outdoors, embarking on imaginative quests, or simply enjoying a quiet moment together, the shared experiences of friendship add depth and color to life's canvas.

Being a good friend also involves the superhero skill of resolving conflicts with grace. Disagreements are a natural part of any relationship, but good friends navigate them with open communication, understanding, and a willingness to find common ground. It's the ability to turn challenges into opportunities for growth, strengthening the bonds of friendship in the process.

So, young adventurers, let the spirit of "Be a Good Friend" guide your interactions with fellow explorers. Whether you're forming new connections, strengthening existing friendships, or navigating the ups and downs of relationships, let kindness, understanding, and shared experiences be your compass.

In the vast adventure of life, being totally American means embracing the beauty of diverse friendships, celebrating individuality, and practicing the art of being a good friend. So, set sail on the seas of camaraderie, my young companions, and let the journey of friendship be a joyful and meaningful part of your quest to be totally American!

Epilogue: Embrace the Adventure

And so, young adventurers, we reach the final chapter of our guide—an epilogue to reflect on the journey of being totally American. As you've explored the diverse landscapes of smiling and saying hi, navigating the whimsical world of American snacks, embracing the tapestry of fashion, igniting school spirit, mastering the art of super slang, celebrating together, being a good sport, speaking up, conquering homework, and fostering meaningful friendships, remember that being totally American is not a destination but a lifelong adventure.

In the great tapestry of America, your unique thread weaves seamlessly into the vibrant mosaic of this nation. As you smile and say hi, share a snack, don your favorite outfit, cheer for your school, speak up in the classroom, persevere through homework, and be a good friend, you contribute to the rich narrative that shapes the American experience.

Embrace the values of teamwork on the sports field, let the words of super slang color your expressions, and relish the joy of celebration with friends and family. Being totally American is about more than just geography; it's a mindset—a celebration of diversity, a commitment to inclusivity, and a recognition that each one of you is an integral part of this incredible journey.

As you embark on the adventure of being totally American, remember the lessons learned in the chapters of this guide. Embrace curiosity, foster resilience, and carry the spirit of kindness in your heart. In the ever-changing landscape of life, your journey is a story waiting to be written—one filled with smiles, shared snacks, laughter, challenges overcome, and friendships that stand the test of time.

So, young adventurers, go forth with confidence, open hearts, and a spirit of exploration. The quest to be totally American is not a checklist but a continuous voyage. Smile, say hi, and let the adventure unfold. The tapestry of America is vast, diverse, and ready to embrace the unique colors you bring to it.

May your journey be filled with joy, discovery, and the knowledge that, in being totally American, you contribute to a story that transcends time and echoes the values of a nation built on dreams, diversity, and the shared pursuit of happiness.

Farewell, young adventurers. Your adventure awaits—embrace it with open arms, and may the spirit of being totally American guide you on this incredible journey called life.

www.ingramcontent.com/pod-product-compliance
Lightning Source LLC
Chambersburg PA
CBHW050751250726
48662CB00005B/2146